THE **BAMBOO TAPE** COLLECTION

TWELVE DESIGNS BY
MARIE WALLIN & MARTIN STOREY
USING **ROWAN BAMBOO TAPE**

D1285602

BAMBOO IS ONE OF THE WORLD'S BEST SUSTAINABLE RESOURCES; IT HOLDS THE RECORD AS THE FASTEST GROWING PLANT, WITH A GROWTH RATE OF UP TO A METER A DAY AND REACHES MATURITY IN 4-5 YEARS. BAMBOO ALSO RE-GROWS FROM OFF-SHOOTS AFTER HARVESTING WITHOUT THE NEED FOR REPLANTING, PESTICIDES OR FERTILIZERS. BAMBOO GRASS TAKES IN NEARLY

5 TIMES THE AMOUNT OF GREENHOUSE GASES AND PRODUCES 35% MORE OXYGEN THAN AN EQUIVALENT STAND OF TREES.

GARMENTS MADE FROM BAMBOO ARE INCREDIBLY SOFT, SMOOTH AND LUXURIOUSLY COMFORTABLE. SOFTER THAN THE SOFTEST COTTON, BAMBOO HAS A NATURAL SHEEN, WONDERFUL DRAPE AND FEELS SIMILAR TO SILK OR CASHMERE NEXT TO YOUR SKIN. DUE TO BAMBOO FIBRE'S CROSS SECTION, WHICH IS COMPOSED OF A MATRIX WITH AIR GAPS, BAMBOO FIBRES ARE EXTREMELY BREATHABLE AND THERMAL REGULATING KEEPING YOU COMFORTABLE IN ALL TEMPERATURES.

MITSU
BY MARIE WALLIN
PATTERN PAGE 48

6

this page
MITSU
BY MARIE WALLIN
PATTERN PAGE 48

opposite
TORI
BY MARIE WALLIN
PATTERN PAGE 52

9

AKINA
BY MARIE WALLIN
PATTERN PAGE 30

KAMEKO
BY MARIE WALLIN
PATTERN PAGE 40

this page
AMAYA
BY MARIE WALLIN
PATTERN PAGE 32

opposite
HARU
BY MARIE WALLIN
PATTERN PAGE 34

KIMI
BY MARIE WALLIN
PATTERN PAGE 42

MARIKO
BY MARIE WALLIN
PATTERN PAGE 46

SAKURA
BY MARIE WALLIN
PATTERN PAGE 50

SIZING GUIDE

Our sizing now conforms to standard clothing sizes. Therefore if you buy a standard size 12 in clothing, then our size 12 or Medium patterns will fit you perfectly.

Dimensions in the charts shown are body measurements, not garment dimensions, therefore please refer to the measuring guide to help you to determine which is the best size for you to knit.

STANDARD SIZING GUIDE FOR WOMEN

UK SIZE	8	10	12	14	16	18	20	22	
USA Size	6	8	10	12	14	16	18	20	
EUR Size	34	36	38	40	42	44	46	48	
To fit bust	32	34	36	38	40	42	44	46	inches
	82	87	92	97	102	107	112	117	cm
To fit waist	24	26	28	30	32	34	36	38	inches
	61	66	71	76	81	86	91	96	cm
To fit hips	34	36	38	40	42	44	46	48	inches
	87	92	97	102	107	112	117	122	cm

CASUAL SIZING GUIDE FOR WOMEN

As there are some designs that are intended to fit more generously, we have introduced our casual sizing guide. The designs that fall into this group can be recognised by the size range: Small, Medium, Large & Xlarge. Each of these sizes cover two sizes from the standard sizing guide, ie. Size S will fit sizes 8/10, size M will fit sizes 12/14 and so on.

The sizing within this chart is also based on the larger size within the range, ie. M will be based on size 14.

	S	M	L	XL	
UK SIZE DUAL SIZE	8/10	12/14	16/18	20/22	
To fit bust	32 – 34	36 – 38	40 – 42	44 – 46	inches
	82 – 87	92 – 97	102 – 107	112 – 117	cm
To fit waist	24 – 26	28 – 30	32 – 34	36 – 38	inches
	61 – 66	71 – 76	81 – 86	91 – 96	cm
To fit hips	34 – 36	38 – 40	42 – 44	46 – 48	inches
	87 – 92	97 – 102	107 – 112	117 – 122	cm

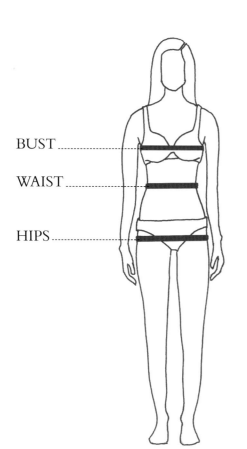

BUST

WAIST

HIPS

MEASURING GUIDE

For maximum comfort and to ensure the correct fit when choosing a size to knit, please follow the tips below when checking your size.

Measure yourself close to your body, over your underwear and don't pull the tape measure too tight!

Bust/chest – measure around the fullest part of the bust/chest and across the shoulder blades.

Waist – measure around the natural waistline, just above the hip bone.

Hips – measure around the fullest part of the bottom. If you don't wish to measure yourself, note the size of a favourite jumper that you like the fit of. Our sizes are now comparable to the clothing sizes from the major high street retailers, so if your favourite jumper is a size Medium or size 12, then our casual size Medium and standard size 12 should be approximately the same fit.

To be extra sure, measure your favourite jumper and then compare these measurements with the Rowan size diagram given at the end of the individual instructions.

Finally, once you have decided which size is best for you, please ensure that you achieve the tension required for the design you wish to knit.

Remember if your tension is too loose, your garment will be bigger than the pattern size and you may use more yarn. If your tension is too tight, your garment could be smaller than the pattern size and you will have yarn left over.

Furthermore if your tension is incorrect, the handle of your fabric will be too stiff or floppy and will not fit properly. It really does make sense to check your tension before starting every project.

GALLERY

MITSU
BY MARIE WALLIN
MAIN IMAGE PAGE 7 & 9
PATTERN PAGE 48

TORI
BY MARIE WALLIN
MAIN IMAGE PAGE 8
PATTERN PAGE 52

AKINA
BY MARIE WALLIN
MAIN IMAGE PAGE 10 & 11
PATTERN PAGE 30

KOSUE
BY MARTIN STOREY
MAIN IMAGE PAGE 12 & 13
PATTERN PAGE 44

KAMEKO
BY MARIE WALLIN
MAIN IMAGE PAGE 14 & 15
PATTERN PAGE 40

SAKURA
BY MARIE WALLIN
MAIN IMAGE PAGE 16 & 26
PATTERN PAGE 50

AMAYA
BY MARIE WALLIN
MAIN IMAGE PAGE 18
PATTERN PAGE 32

HARU
BY MARIE WALLIN
MAIN IMAGE PAGE 19
PATTERN PAGE 34

KIMI
BY MARIE WALLIN
MAIN IMAGE PAGE 20 & 21
PATTERN PAGE 42

HOSHIKO
BY MARIE WALLIN
MAIN IMAGE PAGE 22
PATTERN PAGE 36

SUMI
BY MARIE WALLIN
MAIN IMAGE PAGE 23
PATTERN PAGE 38

MARIKO
BY MARIE WALLIN
MAIN IMAGE PAGE 24 & 25
PATTERN PAGE 46

SIZE KEY　　　■ SIZE 8 – 18　　　● SIZE 8 – 22　　　▲ SIZE S – XL

29

AKINA
BY MARIE WALLIN
MAIN IMAGE PAGE 10 & 11

●

SIZE

	S	M	L	XL	
To fit bust					
	82-87	92-97	102-107	112-117	cm
	32-34	36-38	40-42	44-46	in

YARN
Rowan Bamboo

	12	13	15	16	x 50gm

(photographed in Tissue 709)

NEEDLES
1 pair 4mm (no 8) (US 6) needles
1 pair 5mm (no 6) (US 8) needles

TENSION
19 sts and 27 rows to 10 cm measured over stocking stitch using 5mm (US 8) needles.

BACK
Using 5mm (US 8) needles cast on 89 [99: 109: 121] sts.
Row 1 (RS): K1, *P1, K1, rep from * to end.
Row 2: P1, *K1, P1, rep from * to end.
These 2 rows form rib.

Cont in rib until back meas 29 [30: 31: 32] cm, ending with RS facing for next row.
Shape armholes
Keeping rib correct, cast off 4 [5: 6: 7] sts at beg of next 2 rows. 81 [89: 97: 107] sts.
Dec 1 st at each end of next 3 [5: 5: 7] rows, then on foll 2 [2: 3: 3] alt rows. 71 [75: 81: 87] sts.
Work 5 rows, ending with RS facing for next row.
Beg with a K row, cont in st st until armhole meas 24 [25: 26: 27] cm, ending with RS facing for next row.
Shape shoulders
Cast off 9 [10: 11: 12] sts at beg of next 2 rows, then 9 [10: 11: 13] sts at beg of foll 2 rows.
Cast off rem 35 [35: 37: 37] sts.

LEFT FRONT
Using 5mm (US 8) needles cast on 5 [10: 15: 21] sts.
Row 1 (RS): *K1, P1, rep from * to last 1 [0: 1: 1] st, K1 [0: 1: 1].
Row 2: P1 [0: 1: 1], *K1, P1, rep from * to end.
These 2 rows form rib.
Cont in rib, inc 1 st at end of next row and at same edge on foll 24 rows, then on foll 15 alt rows. 45 [50: 55: 61] sts.

Cont straight until left front matches back to beg of armhole shaping, ending with RS facing for next row.
Shape armhole
Keeping rib correct, cast off 4 [5: 6: 7] sts at beg of next row.
41 [45: 49: 54] sts.
Work 1 row.
Dec 1 st at armhole edge of next 3 [5: 5: 7] rows, then on foll 2 [2: 3: 3] alt rows.
36 [38: 41: 44] sts.
Work 5 rows, ending with RS facing for next row.
Beg with a K row, cont in st st until left front matches back to beg of shoulder shaping, ending with RS facing for next row.
Shape shoulder
Cast off 9 [10: 11: 12] sts at beg of next row, then 9 [10: 11: 13] sts at beg of foll alt row.
Work in st st for a further 9 [9: 9.5: 9.5] cm on rem 18 [18: 19: 19] sts for back neck extension, ending with RS facing for next row.
Cast off.

RIGHT FRONT
Using 5mm (US 8) needles cast on 5 [10: 15: 21] sts.

Row 1 (RS): K1 [0: 1: 1], *P1, K1, rep from * to end.
Row 2: *P1, K1, rep from * to last 1 [0: 1: 1] st, P1 [0: 1: 1].
These 2 rows form rib.
Cont in rib, inc 1 st at beg of next row and at same edge on foll 24 rows, then on foll 15 alt rows. 45 [50: 55: 61] sts.
Complete to match left front, reversing shapings.

SLEEVES
Using 4mm (US 6) needles cast on 53 [55: 57: 57] sts.
Rows 1 and 2: Purl.
Change to 5mm (US 8) needles.
Beg with a K row, work in st st, shaping sides by inc 1 st at each end of 11th [11th: 9th: 7th] and every foll 14th [12th: 10th: 8th] row to 69 [67: 61: 61] sts, then on every foll - [14th: 12th: 10th] row until there are - [73: 77: 81] sts.
Cont straight until sleeve meas 46 [47: 48: 48] cm, ending with RS facing for next row.
Shape top
Cast off 4 [5: 6: 7] sts at beg of next 2 rows.
61 [63: 65: 67] sts.
Dec 1 st at each end of next 9 rows, then on every foll alt row to 35 sts, then on foll 7 rows, ending

with RS facing for next row. 21 sts.
Cast off 4 sts at beg of next 2 rows.
Cast off rem 13 sts.

MAKING UP
Press as described on the information page.

Join both shoulder seams using back stitch, or mattress stitch if preferred. Join cast-off edges of back neck extensions, then sew one edge to back neck cast-off edge.
See information page for finishing instructions, setting in sleeves using the set-in method.

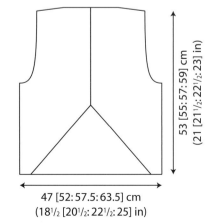

53 [55: 57: 59] cm
(21 [21½: 22½: 23] in)

47 [52: 57.5: 63.5] cm
(18½ [20½: 22½: 25] in)

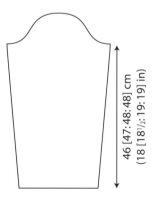

46 [47: 48: 48] cm
(18 [18½: 19: 19] in)

AMAYA
BY MARIE WALLIN
MAIN IMAGE PAGE 18

SIZE

8	10	12	14	16	18	20	22	

To fit bust

82	87	92	97	102	107	112	117	cm
32	34	36	38	40	42	44	46	in

YARN

Rowan Bamboo

9	10	10	11	11	13	13	14	x 50gm

(photographed in Orchid 700)

NEEDLES

1 pair 5mm (no 6) (US 8) needles

TENSION

19 sts and 27 rows to 10 cm measured over stocking stitch using 5mm (US 8) needles.

BACK

Using 5mm (US 8) needles cast on 86 [90: 94: 100: 106: 110: 116: 122] sts.
Row 1 (RS): Purl.
Row 2: Knit.
Beg with a K row, work in st st, dec 1 st at each end of 15th and every foll 6th row until 74 [78: 82: 88: 94: 98: 104: 110] sts rem.
Work 11 rows, ending with RS facing for next row.
Inc 1 st at each end of next and every foll 6th row until there are 82 [86: 90: 96: 102: 106: 112: 118] sts.
Cont straight until back meas 31 [31: 30: 33: 32: 34: 33: 35] cm, ending with RS facing for next row.
Shape for armholes
Cast on 2 sts at beg of next 4 rows, then 4 sts at beg of foll 2 rows.
98 [102: 106: 112: 118: 122: 128: 134] sts.
Cont straight until armhole meas 21 [21: 22: 22: 23: 23: 24: 24] cm from last set of cast-on sts, ending with RS facing for next row.
Shape shoulders and back neck
Cast off 10 [11: 11: 12: 13: 14: 15: 16] sts at beg of next 2 rows.
78 [80: 84: 88: 92: 94: 98: 102] sts.
Next row (RS): Cast off 10 [11: 11: 12: 13: 14: 15: 16] sts, K until there are 14 [14: 16: 17: 17: 17: 18: 19] sts on right needle and turn, leaving rem sts on a holder.
Work each side of neck separately.
Cast off 4 sts at beg of next row.

Cast off rem 10 [10: 12: 13: 13: 13: 14: 15] sts.
With RS facing, rejoin yarn to rem sts, cast off centre 30 [30: 30: 30: 32: 32: 32: 32] sts, K to end.
Complete to match first side, reversing shapings.

FRONT

Work as given for back to beg of armhole shaping.
Shape for armholes and place neck trim
Next row (RS): Cast on 2 sts, K until there are 33 [35: 37: 40: 43: 45: 48: 51] sts on right needle, slip next 20 sts onto a holder for front trim and, in their place, pick up and knit 20 sts behind these sts, K to end.
Cast on 2 sts at beg of next 3 rows, then 4 sts at beg of foll 2 rows.
98 [102: 106: 112: 118: 122: 128: 134] sts.
Cont straight until 36 [36: 36: 38: 38: 38: 40: 40] rows less have been worked than on back to beg of shoulder shaping, ending with RS facing for next row.
Divide for neck
Next row (RS): K47 [49: 51: 54: 57: 59: 62: 65], K2tog and turn, leaving rem sts on a holder.
Work each side of neck separately.
Dec 1 st at neck edge of next 4 [4: 4: 2: 4: 4: 2: 2]

rows, then on every foll alt row until 30 [32: 34: 37: 39: 41: 44: 47] sts rem.

Work 3 rows, ending with RS facing for next row.

Shape shoulder

Cast off 10 [11: 11: 12: 13: 14: 15: 16] sts at beg of next and foll alt row.

Work 1 row.

Cast off rem 10 [10: 12: 13: 13: 13: 14: 15] sts.

With RS facing, rejoin yarn to rem sts, K2tog, K to end.

Complete to match first side, reversing shapings.

MAKING UP

Press as described on the information page.

Join both shoulder seams using back stitch, or mattress stitch if preferred.

Front trim

Slip 20 sts from front holder onto 5mm (US 8) needles and rejoin yarn with RS facing.

Beg with a K row, work in st st for 20 rows, ending with RS facing for next row.

Divide for twist

Next row (RS): K10 and turn, leaving rem sts on a holder.

Work each side of trim separately.

Work in st st on these 10 sts only for a further 71 [71: 75: 75: 79: 79: 81: 81] rows, ending with RS facing for next row.

Cast off.

With RS facing, rejoin yarn to rem sts, K to end.

Complete to match first side.

Using photograph as a guide, twist the 2 front trim pieces together twice, then join cast-off edges. Sew one edge of neck trim to front and back neck edges, positioning twisted section just below beg of front neck shaping.

Armhole borders (both alike)

With RS facing and using 5mm (US 8) needles, beg and ending level with last cast-on set of sts, pick up and knit 78 [78: 82: 82: 86: 86: 90: 90] sts evenly along entire armhole edge.

Cast off knitwise (on **WS**).

See information page for finishing instructions, leaving side seams open for first 8 cm.

54 [54: 54: 57: 57: 59: 59: 61] cm
(21¹/₂ [21¹/₂: 21¹/₂: 22¹/₂: 22¹/₂: 23: 23: 24] in)

43 [45.5: 47.5: 50.5: 53.5: 56: 59: 62] cm
(17 [18: 18¹/₂: 20: 21: 22: 23: 24¹/₂] in)

HARU

BY MARIE WALLIN

MAIN IMAGE PAGE 19

SIZE

	S	M	L	XL	
To fit bust					
	82-87	92-97	102-107	112-117	cm
	32-34	36-38	40-42	44-46	in

YARN

Rowan Bamboo

	11	13	14	16	x 50gm

(photographed in Antique Rose 711)

NEEDLES

1 pair 5mm (no 6) (US 8) needles

TENSION

19 sts and 27 rows to 10 cm measured over stocking stitch using 5mm (US 8) needles.

BACK

Using 5mm (US 8) needles cast on 89 [99: 109: 121] sts.

Row 1 (RS): Purl.

Rows 2 and 3: Knit.

Row 4 (WS): (P2, K1) 4 [4: 5: 6] times, P to last 12 [12: 15: 18] sts, (K1, P2) 4 [4: 5: 6] times.

Row 5: (K2, P1) 4 [4: 5: 6] times, K to last 12 [12: 15: 18] sts, (P1, K2) 4 [4: 5: 6] times.

Rows 4 and 5 form patt.

Work 5 rows, ending with RS facing for next row.

Next row (RS): Patt 12 [12: 15: 18] sts, sl 1, K1, psso, patt to last 14 [14: 17: 20] sts, K2tog, patt to end.

Working all side seam decreases as set by last row, dec 1 st at each end of 8th and every foll 8th row until 81 [91: 101: 113] sts rem.

Work 7 rows, ending with RS facing for next row.

Next row (RS): Patt 12 [12: 15: 18] sts, M1, patt to last 12 [12: 15: 18] sts, M1, patt to end.

Working all side seam increases as set by last row, inc 1 st at each end of 6th and every foll 6th row until there are 89 [99: 109: 121] sts, working inc sts in st st.

Cont straight until back meas 24 [25: 26: 27] cm, ending with RS facing for next row.

Shape armholes

Working all armhole decreases in same way as side seam decreases, dec 1 st at each end of next and every foll 4th row until 65 [69: 75: 81] sts rem.

Cont straight until armhole meas 30 [31: 32: 33] cm, ending with RS facing for next row.

Shape shoulders and back neck

Next row (RS): Cast off 6 [7: 8: 9] sts, patt until there are 10 [11: 12: 14] sts on right needle and turn, leaving rem sts on a holder.

Work each side of neck separately.

Cast off 4 sts at beg of next row.

Cast off rem 6 [7: 8: 10] sts.

With RS facing, rejoin yarn to rem sts, cast off centre 33 [33: 35: 35] sts, patt to end.

Complete to match first side, reversing shapings.

FRONT

Work as given for back to beg of armhole shaping.

Shape armholes

Working all armhole decreases in same way as side seam decreases, dec 1 st at each end of next and every foll 4th row until 77 [85: 95: 105] sts rem.

Work 1 row, ending with RS facing for next row.

Shape neck

Next row (RS): Patt 18 [22: 26: 31] sts and turn, leaving rem sts on a holder.

Work each side of neck separately.

Working all armhole decreases as set, dec 1 st at armhole edge of 2nd and every foll 4th row until 12 [14: 16: 19] sts rem.

Cont straight until front matches back to beg of shoulder shaping, ending with RS facing for next row.

Shape shoulder

Cast off 6 [7: 8: 9] sts at beg of next row.

Work 1 row.

Cast off rem 6 [7: 8: 10] sts.

With RS facing, rejoin yarn to rem sts, cast off centre 41 [41: 43: 43] sts, patt to end.

Complete to match first side, reversing shapings.

SLEEVES

Using 5mm (US 8) needles cast on 129 [133: 137: 141] sts.

Row 1 (RS): Purl.

Row 2: Knit.

Beg with a K row, work in st st for 2 rows, ending with RS facing for next row.

Shape top

Dec 1 st at each end of next and 2 foll 4th rows, then on every foll alt row to 103 sts, then on every row until 29 sts rem, ending with RS facing for next row.

Cast off.

MAKING UP

Press as described on the information page.

Join both shoulder seams using back stitch, or mattress stitch if preferred.

Front neckband

With RS facing and using 5mm (US 8) needles, pick up and knit 41 [41: 44: 44] sts from front neck cast-off edge.

Row 1 (WS): P2, ★K1, P2, rep from ★ to end.

Row 2: K2, ★P1, K2, rep from ★ to end.

Rep last 2 rows 6 times more, ending with **WS** facing for next row.

Cast off in rib (on **WS**).

Sew row-end edges of front neckband to row-end edges of front neck opening.

Join side seams for 14 [15: 16: 17] cm from cast-on edges. Join sleeve seams. Sew sleeves into armholes and along side seam edges.

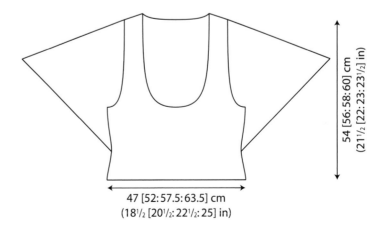

54 [56: 58: 60] cm
(21½ [22: 23: 23½] in)

47 [52: 57.5: 63.5] cm
(18½ [20½: 22½: 25] in)

HOSHIKO

BY MARIE WALLIN

MAIN IMAGE PAGE 22

SIZE

8	10	12	14	16	18	
To fit bust						
82	87	92	97	102	107	cm
32	34	36	38	40	42	in

YARN

Rowan Bamboo

15	15	16	17	17	19	x 50gm

(photographed in Wafer 705)

NEEDLES

1 pair 5mm (no 6) (US 8) needles
5mm (no 6) (US 8) circular needle
5.00mm (no 6) (US H8) crochet hook

BUTTONS - 4 x 417

TENSION

19 sts and 27 rows to 10 cm measured over stocking stitch using 5mm (US 8) needles.

CROCHET ABBREVIATIONS

ch = chain; **dc** = double crochet; **sp** = space;
tr = treble; **dtr** = double treble.

BACK

Using 5mm (US 8) needles cast on 80 [84: 88: 94: 100: 104] sts.
Beg with a K row, work in st st, dec 1 st at each end of 3rd and 2 foll 6th rows.
74 [78: 82: 88: 94: 98] sts.
Cont straight until back meas 9 [9: 8: 11: 10: 12] cm, ending with RS facing for next row.
Inc 1 st at each end of next and every foll 10th row until there are 82 [86: 90: 96: 102: 106] sts.
Work 15 rows, ending with RS facing for next row.
(Back should meas 26 [26: 25: 28: 27: 29] cm.)
Shape armholes
Cast off 5 [6: 6: 7: 7: 8] sts at beg of next 2 rows.
72 [74: 78: 82: 88: 90] sts.
Dec 1 st at each end of next 3 [3: 3: 5: 5: 5] rows, then on foll 1 [1: 2: 1: 2: 2] alt rows.
64 [66: 68: 70: 74: 76] sts.
Cont straight until armhole meas 19 [19: 20: 20: 21: 21] cm, ending with RS facing for next row.
Shape back neck
Next row (RS): K16 [17: 18: 19: 20: 21] and turn, leaving rem sts on a holder.
Work each side of neck separately.
Cast off 3 sts at beg of next row, then 2 sts at beg

of foll alt row, ending with RS facing for next row.
11 [12: 13: 14: 15: 16] sts.
Shape shoulder
Cast off 5 [6: 6: 7: 7: 8] sts at beg of next row.
Work 1 row.
Cast off rem 6 [6: 7: 7: 8: 8] sts.
With RS facing, rejoin yarn to rem sts, cast off centre 32 [32: 32: 32: 34: 34] sts, K to end.
Complete to match first side, reversing shapings.

LEFT FRONT

Using 5mm (US 8) needles cast on 15 [17: 19: 21: 23: 23] sts.
Beg with a K row, work in st st as folls:
Work 1 row, ending with **WS** facing for next row.
Cast on 10 [10: 10: 11: 11: 12] sts at beg of next and foll 3 alt rows, then 7 [8: 9: 9: 10: 10] sts at beg of foll 2 alt rows, and 4 [4: 4: 4: 5: 5] sts at beg of foll 2 alt rows **and at same time** dec 1 st at beg of 2nd and 2 foll 6th rows.
74 [78: 82: 88: 94: 98] sts.
Cont straight until left front meas 9 [9: 8: 11: 10: 12] cm at side seam edge, ending with RS facing for next row.

36

Inc 1 st at each end of next and foll 10th row.
78 [82: 86: 92: 98: 102] sts.
Work 7 rows, ending with RS facing for next row.
Next row (RS): K to last 4 sts, yfwd, K2tog (to make a buttonhole), K2.
Work 1 row.
Inc 1 st at each end of next row, ending with **WS** facing for next row.
80 [84: 88: 94: 100: 104] sts.
Shape front slope
Cast off 12 sts at beg of next and foll alt row, then 6 sts at beg of foll 2 alt rows, and 3 sts at beg of foll 2 alt rows **and at same time** inc 1 st at beg of 10th row.
39 [43: 47: 53: 59: 63] sts.
Dec 1 st at front slope edge of next 3 [3: 5: 5: 5: 5] rows, then on foll 3 [5: 4: 4: 4: 4] alt rows, then on foll 4th [0: 0: 0: 0: 0] row. 32 [35: 38: 44: 50: 54] sts.
Work 1 row, ending with RS facing for next row.
(Left front should now match back to beg of armhole shaping.)
Shape armhole
Cast off 5 [6: 6: 7: 7: 8] sts at beg and dec 0 [1: 1: 1: 1: 1] st at end of next row.
27 [28: 31: 36: 42: 45] sts.
Work 1 row.
Dec 1 st at armhole edge of next 3 [3: 3: 5: 5: 5] rows, then on foll 1 [1: 2: 1: 2: 2] alt rows **and at same time** dec 1 st at front slope edge on next and foll 0 [0: 1: 3: 4: 4] alt rows, then on foll 4th [4th: 4th: 0: 0: 0] row.
21 [22: 23: 26: 30: 33] sts.
Dec 1 st at front slope edge **only** on 4th [4th: 4th: 2nd: 2nd: 2nd] and foll 0 [0: 0: 3: 8: 12] alt rows, then on 8 [8: 8: 7: 5: 3] foll 4th rows, then on foll 6th row.
11 [12: 13: 14: 15: 16] sts.
Cont straight until left front matches back to beg of shoulder shaping, ending with RS facing for next row.
Shape shoulder
Cast off 5 [6: 6: 7: 7: 8] sts at beg of next row.
Work 1 row.
Cast off rem 6 [6: 7: 7: 8: 8] sts.
Mark positions for 3 buttons along side seam edge – top button level with buttonhole already worked, lowest button in row 19, and rem button evenly spaced between.

RIGHT FRONT
Using 5mm (US 8) needles cast on 15 [17: 19: 21: 23: 23] sts.

Beg with a K row, work in st st as folls:
Work 2 rows, ending with RS facing for next row.
Cast on 10 [10: 10: 11: 11: 12] sts at beg of next and foll 3 alt rows, then 7 [8: 9: 9: 10: 10] sts at beg of foll 2 alt rows, and 4 [4: 4: 4: 5: 5] sts at beg of foll 2 alt rows **and at same time** dec 1 st at beg of next and 2 foll 6th rows.
74 [78: 82: 88: 94: 98] sts.
Work 1 row, ending with RS facing for next row.
Row 19 (RS): K2, K2tog, yfwd (to make first buttonhole), K to end.
Complete to match left front, reversing shapings and making a further 2 buttonholes to correspond with positions marked for buttons.

SLEEVES
Using 5mm (US 8) needles cast on 42 [42: 44: 44: 46: 46] sts.
Beg with a K row, work in st st, shaping sides by inc 1 st at each end of 5th and every foll 6th row to 54 [62: 62: 70: 68: 76] sts, then on every foll 8th [8th: 8th: 8th: 8th: –] row until there are 66 [68: 70: 72: 74: –] sts.
Cont straight until sleeve meas 36 [36: 37: 37: 38: 38] cm, ending with RS facing for next row.
Shape top
Cast off 5 [6: 6: 7: 7: 8] sts at beg of next 2 rows.
56 [56: 58: 58: 60: 60] sts.
Dec 1 st at each end of next 7 rows, then on every foll alt row to 30 sts, then on foll 3 rows, ending with RS facing for next row. 24 sts.
Cast off 6 sts at beg of next 2 rows.
Cast off rem 12 sts.

MAKING UP
Press as described on the information page.
Join both shoulder seams using back stitch, or mattress stitch if preferred.
Front edging
With RS facing and using 5mm (US 8) circular needle, pick up and knit 24 [24: 22: 28: 26: 30] sts up right front row-end edge to beg of front slope shaping, 78 [78: 80: 80: 83: 83] sts up right front slope, 44 [44: 44: 44: 46: 46] sts from back, 78 [78: 80: 80: 83: 83] sts down left front slope to beg of front slope shaping, then 24 [24: 22: 28: 26: 30] sts down left front opening edge to cast-on edge.
248 [248: 248: 260: 264: 272] sts.
Cast off knitwise (on **WS**).
Join side seams.
Hem edging
With RS facing and using 5.00mm (US H8)

crochet hook, attach yarn at base of left front opening edge, 1 ch (does NOT count as st), work in dc evenly across entire back and front cast-on edges.
Fasten off.
Hem border
Using 5.00mm (US H8) hook make 22 ch.
Foundation row (RS): 1 dc into 2nd ch from hook, 1 dc into each ch to end, turn. 21 sts.
Cont in patt as folls:
Row 1: 5 ch (counts as first dtr and 1 ch), miss 2 dc, *1 dtr into next dc, 1 ch, miss 1 dc, rep from * to last dc, 1 tr into last dc, turn.
Row 2: 1 ch (does NOT count as st), 1 dc into tr at end of previous row, *1 dc into next ch sp, 1 dc into next dtr, rep from * to end, working last dc into 4th of 5 ch at beg of previous row, turn.

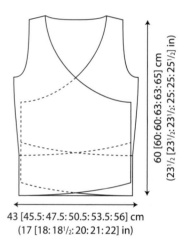

60 [60: 60: 63: 63: 65] cm
(23½ [23½: 23½: 25: 25: 25½] in)

43 [45.5: 47.5: 50.5: 53.5: 56] cm
(17 [18: 18½: 20: 21: 22] in)

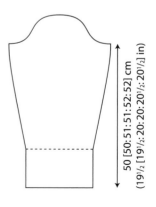

50 [50: 51: 51: 52: 52] cm
(19½ [19½: 20: 20: 20½: 20½] in)

These 2 rows form patt.

Cont in patt until shorter edge of hem border, unstretched, fits along entire hem edge of fronts and back, ending after row 2.

Fasten off.

Slip stitch hem border in place.

Sleeve edgings (both alike)

With RS facing and using 5.00mm (US H8) crochet hook, attach yarn to cast-on edge of sleeve, 1 ch (does NOT count as st), work in dc evenly across cast-on edge.

Fasten off.

Cuff borders (both alike)

Work as given for hem border, making a strip to fit

across cast-on edge of sleeve, ending after row 2.

Fasten off.

Slip stitch cuff borders in place.

See information page for finishing instructions, setting in sleeves using the set-in method and attaching buttons 5 cm below marked positions (so that right front drops).

SUMI
BY MARIE WALLIN
MAIN IMAGE PAGE 23

SIZE

	S	M	L	XL	
To fit bust					
	82-87	92-97	102-107	112-117	cm
	32-34	36-38	40-42	44-46	in

YARN

Rowan Bamboo

	9	10	11	12	x 50gm

(photographed in Chalk 703)

NEEDLES

1 pair 4½mm (no 7) (US 7) needles

1 pair 5mm (no 6) (US 8) needles

TENSION

19 sts and 27 rows to 10 cm measured over stocking stitch using 5mm (US 8) needles.

BACK

Using 4½mm (US 7) needles cast on 87 [97: 107: 119] sts.

Row 1 (RS): K1, *P1, K1, rep from * to end.

Row 2: As row 1.

These 2 rows form moss st.

Work in moss st for a further 6 rows, dec 1 st at centre of last row and ending with RS facing for next row.

86 [96: 106: 118] sts.
Change to 5mm (US 8) needles.
Next row (RS): Moss st 6 sts, K to last 6 sts, moss st 6 sts.
Next row: Moss st 6 sts, P to last 6 sts, moss st 6 sts.
Rep last 2 rows 6 times more.
Beg with a K row, cont in st st, dec 1 st at each end of 3rd and every foll 8th row until 78 [88: 98: 110] sts rem.
Work 15 rows, ending with RS facing for next row.
Inc 1 st at each end of next and every foll 8th row until there are 84 [94: 104: 116] sts.
Cont straight until work meas 38 [39: 40: 41] cm, ending with RS facing for next row.★★
Cast off.

FRONT
Work as given for back to ★★.
Shape for armholes
Cast off 7 [8: 9: 10] sts at beg of next 2 rows.
70 [78: 86: 96] sts.
Dec 1 st at each end of next 9 [11: 11: 13] rows, then on foll 3 [3: 4: 4] alt rows, then on foll 4th row.
44 [48: 54: 60] sts.
Work 3 rows, dec 1 st at centre of last row and ending with RS facing for next row.
43 [47: 53: 59] sts.

Change to 4½mm (US 7) needles.
Work in moss st for 8 rows, ending with RS facing for next row.
Cast off in moss st.

MAKING UP
Press as described on the information page.
Join side seams using back stitch, or mattress stitch if preferred, leaving seams open for first 22 rows.
Halter strap
Using 4½mm (US 7) needles cast on 10 sts.
Row 1 (RS): (K1, P1) 5 times.
Row 2: (P1, K1) 5 times.
These 2 rows form moss st.
Cont in moss st until strap, when slightly stretched, fits from centre back, across cast-off edge of back and up front armhole edge to front cast-off edge.
Mark ends of last row.
Work in moss st until strap meas 44 [44: 46: 46] cm from markers.
Mark ends of last row.
Cont in moss st until strap, from second marked row and when slightly stretched, fits down other front armhole edge to side seam, then across back cast-off edge to centre back, ending with RS facing for next row.
Cast off in moss st.
Join cast-off and cast-on ends of strap, then slip stitch strap in place, leaving centre section free

between markers.
Belt
Using 4½mm (US 7) needles cast on 10 sts.
Work in moss st as given for strap until belt meas 120 [130: 140: 150] cm, ending with RS facing for next row.
Cast off in moss st.

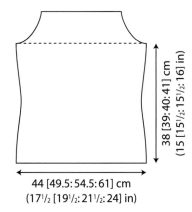

38 [39: 40: 41] cm
(15 [15½: 15½: 16] in)

44 [49.5: 54.5: 61] cm
(17½ [19½: 21½: 24] in)

KAMEKO

BY MARIE WALLIN

MAIN IMAGE PAGE 14 & 15

SIZE

	S	M	L	XL	
To fit bust					
	82-87	92-97	102-107	112-117	cm
	32-34	36-38	40-42	44-46	in

YARN

Rowan Bamboo

A Wafer 705

| | 6 | 7 | 8 | 9 | x 50gm |

B Lolly 704

| | 3 | 3 | 4 | 4 | x 50gm |

NEEDLES

1 pair 5mm (no 6) (US 8) needles
5.00mm (no 6) (US H8) crochet hook

BUTTONS - 2 x 417

TENSION

19 sts and 27 rows to 10 cm measured over
stocking stitch using 5mm (US 8) needles.

CROCHET ABBREVIATIONS

ch = chain; **dc** = double crochet; **sp** = space.

BACK

Using 5mm (US 8) needles and yarn A cast on 84
[94: 104: 116] sts.
Row 1 (RS): Purl.
Rows 2 to 4: Knit.
Beg with a K row, work in st st, dec 1 st at each
end of 17th and every foll 10th row until 78 [88:
98: 110] sts rem.
Work 19 rows, ending with RS facing for next
row.
Inc 1 st at each end of next and every foll 10th
row until there are 84 [94: 104: 116] sts.
Cont straight until back meas 35 [36: 37: 38] cm,
ending with RS facing for next row.
Shape armholes
Cast off 7 [8: 9: 10] sts at beg of next 2 rows.
70 [78: 86: 96] sts.★★
Dec 1 st at each end of next 3 [5: 7: 9] rows, then
on foll 5 [5: 4: 4] alt rows.
54 [58: 64: 70] sts.
Cont straight until armhole meas 13 [14: 15: 16]
cm, ending with RS facing for next row.
Shape back neck
Next row (RS): K17 [19: 21: 24] and turn,
leaving rem sts on a holder.

Work each side of neck separately.
Dec 1 st at neck edge of next 9 rows.
8 [10: 12: 15] sts.
Work 4 rows, ending with RS facing for next row.
Shape shoulder
Cast off rem 8 [10: 12: 15] sts.
With RS facing, rejoin yarn to rem sts, cast off
centre 20 [20: 22: 22] sts, K to end.
Complete to match first side, reversing shapings.

FRONT

Work as given for back to ★★.
Dec 1 st at each end of next 3 [4: 4: 4] rows.
64 [70: 78: 88] sts.
Work 1 [0: 0: 0] row, ending with RS facing for
next row.
Shape front neck
Next row (RS): K2tog, K23 [26: 29: 34] and
turn, leaving rem sts on a holder.
Work each side of neck separately.
Dec 1 st at neck edge of next 8 rows, then on foll
4 alt rows **and at same time** dec 1 st at armhole
edge of 2nd [2nd: next: next] and foll 0 [0: 1: 3]
rows, then on foll 3 [4: 4: 4] alt rows.
8 [10: 12: 15] sts.

Cont straight until front matches back to shoulder cast-off, ending with RS facing for next row.

Shape shoulder

Cast off rem 8 [10: 12: 15] sts.

With RS facing, rejoin yarn to rem sts, cast off centre 14 [14: 16: 16] sts, K to last 2 sts, K2tog.

Complete to match first side, reversing shapings.

LEFT FRONT OVERLAY

Using 5mm (US 8) needles and yarn B cast on 57 [62: 67: 73] sts.

Row 1 (RS): K4 [3: 2: 2], *P1, K5, rep from * to last 5 sts, P1, K4.

Row 2: P4, K1, *P5, K1, rep from * to last 4 [3: 2: 2] sts, P4 [3: 2: 2].

These 2 rows form patt.

Cont in patt, inc 1 st at beg of 5th and foll alt row, taking inc sts into patt.

59 [64: 69: 75] sts.

Work 1 row, ending with RS facing for next row.

Shape armhole

Keeping patt correct, cast off 12 [13: 14: 15] sts at beg of next row, then 3 sts at beg of foll 4 alt rows.

35 [39: 43: 48] sts.

Work 1 row, ending with RS facing for next row.

Dec 1 st at beg of next and foll 11 [16: 21: 28] alt rows, then on 7 [6: 5: 3] foll 4th rows, then on every foll 6th row until 8 sts rem.

Cont straight until left front overlay meas 50 [52: 55: 57] cm from cast-on edge, ending with RS facing for next row.

Cast off.

RIGHT FRONT OVERLAY

Using 5mm (US 8) needles and yarn B cast on 57 [62: 67: 73] sts.

Row 1 (RS): K4, P1, *K5, P1, rep from * to last 4 [3: 2: 2] sts, K4 [3: 2: 2].

Row 2: P4 [3: 2: 2], *K1, P5, rep from * to last 5 sts, K1, P4.

These 2 rows form patt.

Cont in patt, inc 1 st at end of 5th and foll alt row, taking inc sts into patt.

59 [64: 69: 75] sts.

Complete to match left front overlay, reversing shapings.

MAKING UP

Press as described on the information page.

Join right shoulder seam using back stitch, or mattress stitch if preferred.

Neckband

With RS facing, using 5mm (US 8) needles and yarn A, pick up and knit 34 [36: 38: 40] sts down left side of front neck, 14 [14: 16: 16] sts from front, 34 [36: 38: 40] sts up right side of front neck, 11 sts down right side of back neck, 20 [20: 22: 22] sts from back, then 11 sts up left side of back neck. 124 [128: 136: 140] sts.

Cast off knitwise (on **WS**).

Join left shoulder and neckband seam.

Armhole borders (both alike)

With RS facing, using 5mm (US 8) needles and yarn A, pick up and knit 94 [100: 106: 112] sts evenly around armhole edge.

Cast off knitwise (on **WS**).

See information page for finishing instructions. Attach buttons to front, placing buttons 10 cm up from cast-on edge and 2.5 cm forward from side seams.

Front overlay ties (both alike)

Mark points along straight front opening edges of overlay pieces 8 cm and 17 cm up from cast-on edge.

With RS facing, using 5mm (US 8) needles and yarn B, pick up and knit 28 sts between marked points.

Beg with a P row, work in st st, dec 1 st at each end of 4th and every foll 4th row until there are 18 sts, then on every foll alt row until 6 sts rem. Cont straight until tie meas 40 cm from pick-up row, ending with RS facing for next row.

Cast off.

Overlay buttonhole bands (both alike)

With RS facing, using 5.00mm (US H8) crochet hook and yarn B, attach yarn and work 7 dc evenly along shaped side seam row-end edge of overlay, turn.

Row 1 (WS): 1 ch (does NOT count as st), 1 dc into each dc to end, turn.

Row 2: As row 1.

Row 3: 1 ch (does NOT count as st), 1 dc into each of first 3 dc, 1 ch, miss 1 dc (to make a buttonhole), 1 dc into each of last 3 dc, turn.

Row 4: 1 ch (does NOT count as st), 1 dc into each of first 3 dc, 1 dc into next ch sp, 1 dc into each of last 3 dc.

Fasten off.

Join centre back neck seam of front overlay pieces by joining cast-off edges.

Overlay lower and armhole edging

With RS facing, using 5.00mm (US H8) crochet hook and yarn B, attach yarn to left front overlay at lower edge of overlay tie, 1 ch (does NOT count as st), work in dc evenly around entire hem, side seam and armhole/back neck edges to lower edge of right front overlay tie, working 3 dc into each corner point, turn.

Next row (WS): 1 ch (does NOT count as st), 1 dc into each dc to end, working 3 dc into each corner point.

Fasten off.

Overlay neck edging

With RS facing, using 5.00mm (US H8) crochet hook and yarn B, attach yarn to right front overlay at upper edge of overlay tie, 1 ch (does NOT count as st), work in dc evenly along entire front opening and back neck edge, turn.

Next row (WS): 1 ch (does NOT count as st), 1 dc into each dc to end.

Fasten off.

Using yarn A and photograph as a guide, work lines of running stitch up each "P" st of patt of overlay pieces, working each st over and under 2 rows.

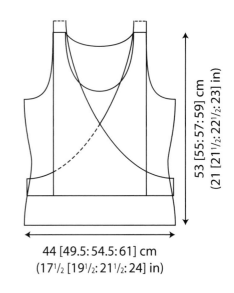

53 [55: 57: 59] cm
(21 [21½: 22½: 23] in)

44 [49.5: 54.5: 61] cm
(17½ [19½: 21½: 24] in)

KIMI

BY MARIE WALLIN

MAIN IMAGE PAGE 20 & 21

●

SIZE

	S	M	L	XL	
To fit bust					
	82-87	92-97	102-107	112-117	cm
	32-34	36-38	40-42	44-46	in

YARN

Rowan Bamboo

	12	14	15	17	x 50gm

(photographed in Wode 708)

NEEDLES

1 pair 5mm (no 6) (US 8) needles

TENSION

19 sts and 27 rows to 10 cm measured over stocking stitch using 5mm (US 8) needles.

LOWER BACK

Using 5mm (US 8) needles cast on 61 [67: 75: 83] sts.
Row 1 (RS): K1, *P1, K1, rep from * to end.
Row 2: P1, *K1, P1, rep from * to end.
These 2 rows form rib.
Work in rib for a further 6 rows, ending with RS facing for next row.

Row 9 (RS): Knit.
Row 10: K1, P to last st, K1.
These 2 rows set the sts.
Cont as set until lower back meas 24 [25: 26: 27] cm, ending with RS facing for next row.
Cast off.

UPPER BACK

Using 5mm (US 8) needles cast on 61 [67: 75: 83] sts.
Row 1 (RS): Knit.
Row 2: K1, P to last st, K1.
These 2 rows set the sts.
Keeping sts correct as set, work 4 rows, ending with RS facing for next row.
Row 7 (RS): K1, M1, K to last st, M1, K1.
Working all increases as set by last row, inc 1 st at each end of 6th and every foll 6th row until there are 71 [77: 85: 93] sts.
Cont straight until upper back meas 16 [17: 18: 19] cm, ending with RS facing for next row.
Shape shoulders
Cast off 7 [8: 10: 12] sts at beg of next 2 rows, then 7 [9: 10: 12] sts at beg of foll 2 rows.
Cast off rem 43 [43: 45: 45] sts.

LEFT FRONT

Using 5mm (US 8) needles cast on 79 [81: 85: 89] sts.
Row 1 (RS): Purl.
Rows 2 and 3: Knit.
Row 4: K1, P to last st, K1.
Rows 3 and 4 set the sts.
Cont as set until left front meas 26 [27: 28: 29] cm, ending with RS facing for next row.
Working all increases in same way as given for upper back increases, inc 1 st at beg of next and every foll 6th row until there are 84 [86: 90: 94] sts.
Cont straight until left front meas 37 [39: 41: 43] cm, ending with **WS** facing for next row.
Shape neck
Cast off 66 [65: 66: 66] sts at beg of next row. 18 [21: 24: 28] sts.
Dec 1 st at neck edge of next 4 rows. 14 [17: 20: 24] sts.
Work 3 rows, ending with RS facing for next row.
Shape shoulders
Cast off 7 [8: 10: 12] sts at beg of next row.
Work 1 row.
Cast off rem 7 [9: 10: 12] sts.

RIGHT FRONT

Using 5mm (US 8) needles cast on 79 [81: 85: 89] sts.

Row 1 (RS): Purl.
Rows 2 and 3: Knit.
Row 4: K1, P to last st, K1.
Rows 3 and 4 set the sts.
Cont as set until right front meas 26 [27: 28: 29] cm, ending with RS facing for next row.
Working all increases in same way as given for upper back increases, inc 1 st at end of next and every foll 6th row until there are 84 [86: 90: 94] sts.
Complete to match left front, reversing shapings.

CENTRE SLEEVE PANEL
Using 5mm (US 8) needles cast on 25 [29: 33: 35] sts.
Row 1 (RS): Knit.
Row 2: K1, P to last st, K1.
These 2 rows set the sts.
Cont as set until centre sleeve panel meas 23 [24: 25: 26] cm, ending with RS facing for next row.
Dec 1 st at each end of next 10 [10: 12: 12] rows, ending with RS facing for next row.
Cast off rem 5 [9: 9: 11] sts.

LEFT FRONT SIDE PANEL
Using 5mm (US 8) needles cast on 17 [19: 19: 21] sts.
Work in rib as given for lower back for 8 rows, inc 0 [0: 1: 1] st at centre of last row and ending with RS facing for next row. 17 [19: 20: 22] sts.
Row 1 (RS): Knit.
Row 2: K1, P to last st, K1.
These 2 rows set the sts.
Keeping sts correct as set and working all increases as set by upper back, inc 1 st at end (body edge) of 3rd and 13 foll 4th rows **and at same time** inc 1 st at beg (side seam/armhole edge) of 11th and 13 foll 4th rows. 45 [47: 48: 50] sts.
Cont straight until left front side panel meas 33

[34: 35: 36] cm, ending with RS facing for next row.
Cast off.

RIGHT BACK SIDE PANEL
Work as given for left front side panel.

RIGHT FRONT AND LEFT BACK SIDE PANELS
Work as given for left front side panel, reversing shapings.

MAKING UP
Press as described on the information page.
Join all seams using back stitch and holding pieces **WS** facing, so that seams form ridges on RS of garment, as folls:
Sew cast-off edge of lower back to cast-on edge of

upper back. Join shoulder seams. Sew cast-off edges of side panels to row-end edges of centre sleeve panels, positioning cast-on edge of centre sleeve panel at side seam/armhole edge of side panels.
Ties (make 2)
Using 5mm (US 8) needles cast on 5 sts.
Work in rib as given for lower back until tie meas 50 [55: 60: 65] cm, ending with RS facing for next row.
Cast off in rib.
Matching centre of cast-off edge of centre sleeve panel to shoulder seam and cast-on edges of side panels to cast-on edges of lower back and fronts, sew centre sleeve and side panels to backs and fronts, enclosing end of tie in back seam approx 2 cm up from cast-on edge. Join side seams for first 17 [18: 19: 20] cm.

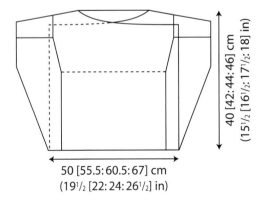

50 [55.5: 60.5: 67] cm
(19½ [22: 24: 26½] in)

40 [42: 44: 46] cm
(15½ [16½: 17½: 18] in)

KOSUE

BY MARTIN STOREY

MAIN IMAGE PAGE 12 & 13

SIZE

8	10	12	14	16	18	20	22	
To fit bust								
82	87	92	97	102	107	112	117	cm
32	34	36	38	40	42	44	46	in

YARN

Rowan Bamboo

9	9	10	10	11	12	12	13	x 50gm

(photographed in Sherbet 702)

NEEDLES

1 pair 4½mm (no 7) (US 7) needles
1 pair 5mm (no 6) (US 8) needles

TENSION

19 sts and 27 rows to 10 cm measured over stocking stitch using 5mm (US 8) needles.

BACK

Using 4½mm (US 7) needles cast on 77 [81: 85: 91: 97: 103: 107: 115] sts.
Work in g st for 4 rows, ending with RS facing for next row.
Change to 5mm (US 8) needles.

Beg with a K row, work in st st, dec 1 st at each end of 9th and every foll 6th row until 69 [73: 77: 83: 89: 95: 99: 107] sts rem.
Cont straight until back meas 14 [14: 13: 16: 15: 17: 16: 18] cm, ending with RS facing for next row.
Inc 1 st at each end of next and foll 10th row, then on every foll 12th row until there are 77 [81: 85: 91: 97: 103: 107: 115] sts.
Work 9 rows, ending with RS facing for next row. (Back should meas 30 [30: 29: 32: 31: 33: 32: 34] cm.)
Change to 4½mm (US 7) needles.
Work in g st for 3 rows, ending with **WS** facing for next row.
Cast off knitwise (on **WS**).

LEFT FRONT

Using 4½mm (US 7) needles cast on 63 [65: 67: 70: 73: 76: 78: 82] sts.
Work in g st for 4 rows, ending with RS facing for next row.
Change to 5mm (US 8) needles.
Beg with a K row, work in st st, dec 1 st at beg of 9th and every foll 6th row until 59 [61: 63: 66: 69: 72: 74: 78] sts rem.

Cont straight until 4 rows less have been worked than on back to first side seam inc, ending with RS facing for next row.

Shape front slope

Dec 1 st at end of next and foll 21 [21: 20: 20: 21: 21: 19: 19] alt rows, then on 1 [1: 2: 2: 1: 1: 2: 2] foll 4th rows **and at same time** inc 1 st at beg of 5th and foll 10th row, then on 2 foll 12th rows.
40 [42: 44: 47: 50: 53: 56: 60] sts.
Work 3 [3: 1: 1: 3: 3: 3: 3] rows, ending with RS facing for next row.

Shape armhole

Cast off 5 [6: 6: 7: 7: 8: 8: 9] sts at beg and dec 1 [1: 0: 0: 1: 1: 1: 1] st at end of next row.
34 [35: 38: 40: 42: 44: 47: 50] sts.
Work 1 row.
Dec 1 st at armhole edge of next 7 [7: 9: 9: 11: 11: 13: 13] rows, then on foll 6 [8: 8: 12: 12: 16: 15: 21] alt rows, then on 7 [6: 6: 4: 4: 2: 3: 0] foll 4th rows **and at same time** dec 1 st at front slope edge of 3rd [3rd: next: next: 3rd: 3rd: 3rd: 3rd] and every foll 4th row.
2 sts.
Work 3 rows, ending with RS facing for next row.
Next row (RS): K2tog and fasten off.

RIGHT FRONT

Using 4½mm (US 7) needles cast on 63 [65: 67: 70: 73: 76: 78: 82] sts.

Work in g st for 4 rows, ending with RS facing for next row.

Change to 5mm (US 8) needles.

Beg with a K row, work in st st, dec 1 st at end of 9th and every foll 6th row until 59 [61: 63: 66: 69: 72: 74: 78] sts rem.

Complete to match left front, reversing shapings.

MAKING UP

Press as described on the information page.

Front armhole borders (both alike)

With RS facing and using 4½mm (US 7) needles, pick up and knit 44 [45: 47: 48: 50: 51: 55: 56] sts evenly along armhole edge, between fasten-off point and top of side seam.

Cast off knitwise (on **WS**).

Place markers along front slopes 13 cm below fasten-off points.

Left front band and collar

Using 4½mm (US 7) needles cast on 3 sts.

Work in g st until band, when slightly stretched, fits up left front opening edge to beg of front slope shaping, ending with RS facing for next row.

Shape for collar

Inc 1 st at beg of next and foll 8 alt rows, then on every foll 4th row until there are 22 sts.

Cont straight until collar section, unstretched, fits up front slope to marked point, ending with **WS** facing for next row.

Next row (WS): Cast off 9 sts, then cast on 9 sts, K to end. 22 sts.

Cont straight until collar section, unstretched, fits up front slope to fasten-off point.

Cont in g st for a further 6 [6: 6: 6: 6.5: 6.5: 6.5: 6.5] cm, ending with RS facing for next row. Cast off.

Right front band and collar

Work to match left front band and collar, reversing shapings.

Join cast-off ends of collar sections, then slip stitch bands and collars in place.

Ties (make 2)

Using 4½mm (US 7) needles cast on 7 sts.

Row 1 (RS): sl 1, K6.

Row 2: As row 1.

Rep these 2 rows until tie meas 102 cm, ending with RS facing for next row.

Cast off.

Matching cast-off edges, join both side seams using back stitch, or mattress stitch if preferred, leaving a small opening in right side seam level with beg of front slope shaping. Attach ties to front opening edges level with beg of front slope shaping.

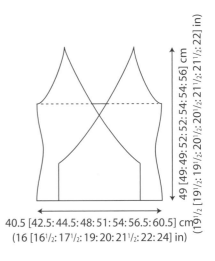

40.5 [42.5: 44.5: 48: 51: 54: 56.5: 60.5] cm
(16 [16½: 17½: 19: 20: 21½: 22: 24] in)

49 [49: 49: 52: 52: 54: 54: 56] cm
(19½ [19½: 19½: 20½: 20½: 21½: 21½: 22] in)

MARIKO
BY MARIE WALLIN
MAIN IMAGE PAGE 24 & 25

SIZE

	S	M	L	XL	
To fit bust					
	82-87	92-97	102-107	112-117	cm
	32-34	36-38	40-42	44-46	in

YARN
Rowan Bamboo

10	12	13	14	x 50gm

(photographed in Amethyst 710)

NEEDLES
1 pair 5mm (no 6) (US 8) needles
4mm (no 8) (US 6) circular needle

BUTTONS - 2 x 407

RIBBON – 1.50 m of 2.5cm wide organza ribbon

TENSION
19 sts and 27 rows to 10 cm measured over stocking stitch using 5mm (US 8) needles.

BACK
Using 5mm (US 8) needles cast on 89 [99: 109: 121] sts.
Beg with a K row, work in st st, dec 1 st at each end of 15th and every foll 8th row until 79 [89: 99: 111] sts rem.
Work 11 rows, ending with RS facing for next row.
Inc 1 st at each end of next and every foll 8th row until there are 89 [99: 109: 121] sts.
Work 2 rows, ending with **WS** facing for next row.

Form back casing
Next row (WS): P75 [83: 92: 102] and turn, leaving rem 14 [16: 17: 19] sts on a holder.
Next row: K61 [67: 75: 83] and turn, leaving rem 14 [16: 17: 19] sts on a second holder.
Work 6 rows on these 61 [67: 75: 83] sts, ending with **WS** facing for next row.
Next row (WS): ★Pick up st 7 rows directly below next st on left needle and place on left needle, P tog this picked-up st with next st on left needle, rep from ★ 60 [66: 74: 82] times more, then P 14 [16: 17: 19] sts on first holder.
Next row: K to end, then K 14 [16: 17: 19] sts on second holder.
89 [99: 109: 121] sts.

Cont straight until work meas 39 [40: 41: 42] cm, ending with RS facing for next row.

Shape armholes
Place markers at both ends of last row to denote base of armhole openings.
Next row (RS): K2, M1, K to last 2 sts, M1, K2.
Next row: K2, P to last 2 sts, K2.
These 2 rows set the sts and armhole increases.
Cont as set, inc 1 st at each end of next and every foll 4th row until there are 101 [111: 121: 133] sts.
Cont straight until armhole meas 12 [13: 14: 15] **cm from markers**, ending with RS facing for next row.

Shape back neck
Next row (RS): Knit.
Next row: K2, P27 [32: 36: 42], K43 [43: 45: 45], P to last 2 sts, K2.
Rep last 2 rows once more, ending with RS facing for next row.
Next row (RS): K31 [36: 40: 46] and turn, leaving rem sts on a holder.
Work each side of neck separately.
Next row (WS): K2, P to last 2 sts, K2.
Next row: Knit.
Rep last 2 rows until armhole meas 21 [22: 23: 24]

cm **from markers**, ending with RS facing for next row.

Shape shoulder

Cast off 15 [18: 20: 23] sts at beg of next row.

Work 1 row.

Cast off rem 16 [18: 20: 23] sts.

With RS facing, rejoin yarn to rem sts, cast off centre 39 [39: 41: 41] sts, K to end.

Complete to match first side, reversing shapings.

LEFT FRONT

Using 5mm (US 8) needles cast on 7 [12: 17: 23] sts.

Beg with a K row, work in st st as folls:

Work 1 row, ending with **WS** facing for next row.

Cast on 5 sts at beg of next and foll 2 alt rows, then 4 sts at beg of foll 4 alt rows, and 3 sts at beg of foll 3 alt rows **and at same time** dec 1 st at beg of 14th row. 46 [51: 56: 62] sts.

Work 1 row, ending with **WS** facing for next row.

Inc 1 st at beg of next row and at same edge on foll 5 rows **and at same time** dec 1 st at beg of 2nd row. 51 [56: 61: 67] sts.

Next row (WS): K2, P to end.

Next row: Knit.

These 2 rows set the sts.

Keeping sts correct as now set, dec 1 st at beg of 2nd and 2 foll 8th rows. 48 [53: 58: 64] sts.

Work 11 rows, ending with RS facing for next row.

Inc 1 st at beg of next and every foll 8th row until there are 53 [58: 63: 69] sts.

Cont straight until 8 rows less have been worked than on back to beg of armhole shaping, ending with RS facing for next row.

Shape front slope

Next row (RS): K to last 3 sts, K2tog, K1.

Working all front slope decreases as set by last row, dec 1 st at front slope edge of 2nd and foll 2 alt rows.

49 [54: 59: 65] sts.

Work 1 row, ending with RS facing for next row.

Shape armhole

Place markers at end of last row to denote base of armhole openings.

Next row (RS): K2, M1, K to last 3 sts, K2tog, K1.

Next row: K2, P to last 2 sts, K2.

These 2 rows set the sts and armhole increases.

Cont as set, inc 1 st at armhole edge of next and 4 foll 4th rows **and at same time** dec 1 st at front slope edge of next and every foll alt row.

45 [50: 55: 61] sts.

Dec 1 st at front slope edge **only** on 2nd and foll 12 [10: 11: 10] alt rows, then on every foll 4th row until 31 [36: 40: 46] sts rem.

Cont straight until left front matches back to beg of shoulder shaping, ending with RS facing for next row.

Shape shoulder

Cast off 15 [18: 20: 23] sts at beg of next row.

Work 1 row.

Cast off rem 16 [18: 20: 23] sts.

RIGHT FRONT

Using 5mm (US 8) needles cast on 7 [12: 17: 23] sts.

Beg with a K row, work in st st as folls:

Work 2 rows, ending with RS facing for next row.

Cast on 5 sts at beg of next and foll 2 alt rows, then 4 sts at beg of foll 4 alt rows, and 3 sts at beg of foll 3 alt rows **and at same time** dec 1 st at end of 13th row.

46 [51: 56: 62] sts.

Inc 1 st at end of next row and at same edge on foll 5 rows **and at same time** dec 1 st at end of 2nd row. 51 [56: 61: 67] sts.

Next row (WS): P to last 2 sts, K2.

Next row: Knit.

These 2 rows set the sts.

Keeping sts correct as now set, complete to match left front, reversing shapings.

MAKING UP

Press as described on the information page.

Join both shoulder seams using back stitch, or mattress stitch if preferred. Join side seams below markers.

Hem border

With RS facing and using 4mm (US 6) circular needle, beg and ending at base of front opening edges, pick up and knit 55 [60: 65: 71] sts along shaped inc and cast-on edge of left front, 89 [99: 109: 121] sts across back cast-on edge, then 55 [60: 65: 71] sts along shaped cast-on and inc edge of right front.

199 [219: 239: 263] sts.

Work in g st for 2 rows, ending with **WS** facing for next row.

Cast off knitwise (on **WS**).

Overlap front opening edges by 17 sts and attach first button to left front, positioning it level with beg of right front slope shaping. Attach second button to right front 3 cm in from front opening edge and 7cm below beg of front slope shaping.

Cut 50cm length of yarn and knot through right front opening edge level with beg of front slope shaping. Fasten garment by wrapping this length of yarn around button attached to left front.

Cut ribbon into 2 equal lengths and thread both lengths through back casing. Tie ends of ribbon in bows at each end of casing, pulling up casing so back is slightly gathered and ensuring knots of bows are large enough not to slip inside casing.

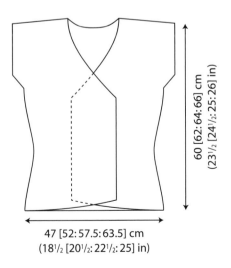

60 [62: 64: 66] cm
(23½ [24½: 25: 26] in)

47 [52: 57.5: 63.5] cm
(18½ [20½: 22½: 25] in)

MITSU

BY MARIE WALLIN

MAIN IMAGE PAGE 7 & 9

●●

SIZE

	S	M	L	XL	
To fit bust					
	82-87	92-97	102-107	112-117	cm
	32-34	36-38	40-42	44-46	in

YARN

Rowan Bamboo

16	18	20	21	x 50gm

(photographed in Wedgewood 707)

NEEDLES

1 pair 5mm (no 6) (US 8) needles
5.00mm (no 6) (US H8) crochet hook

TENSION

19 sts and 27 rows to 10 cm measured over
stocking stitch using 5mm (US 8) needles.

CROCHET ABBREVIATIONS

ch = chain; **dc** = double crochet.

BACK

Using 5mm (US 8) needles cast on 89 [99:
109: 121] sts.

Row 1 (RS): Purl.
Row 2: Knit.
Beg with a K row, cont in st st, dec 1 st at each
end of 19th [21st: 25th: 27th] and foll 20th row.
85 [95: 105: 117] sts.
Work 15 rows, ending with RS facing for next row.
Inc 1 st at each end of next and foll 20th row.
89 [99: 109: 121] sts.
Work 17 rows, ending with RS facing for next
row. (Back should meas 35 [36: 37: 38] cm.)
Shape armholes
Cast off 3 [4: 5: 6] sts at beg of next 2 rows.
83 [91: 99: 109] sts.
Dec 1 st at each end of next 1 [3: 3: 5] rows, then
on foll 2 [2: 3: 3] alt rows. 77 [81: 87: 93] sts.
Cont straight until armhole meas 22 [23: 24: 25] cm,
ending with RS facing for next row.
Shape back neck
Next row (RS): K21 [23: 25: 28] and turn,
leaving rem sts on a holder.
Work each side of neck separately.
Dec 1 st at neck edge of next 3 rows, ending with
RS facing for next row. 18 [20: 22: 25] sts.
Shape shoulder
Cast off 6 [7: 7: 8] sts at beg of next and foll alt row.

Work 1 row.
Cast off rem 6 [6: 8: 9] sts.
With RS facing, rejoin yarn to rem sts, cast off
centre 35 [35: 37: 37] sts, K to end.
Complete to match first side, reversing shapings.

LEFT FRONT

Using 5mm (US 8) needles cast on 59 [64: 69: 75] sts.
Row 1 (RS): Purl.
Row 2: Knit.
Beg with a K row, cont in st st, dec 1 st at beg of
19th [21st: 25th: 27th] and foll 20th row. 57 [62:
67: 73] sts.
Work 15 rows, ending with RS facing for next
row.
Inc 1 st at beg of next row. 58 [63: 68: 74] sts.
Work 11 rows, ending with RS facing for next
row.
Shape front slope
Dec 1 st at end of next and 6 foll 4th rows and at
same time inc 1 st at beg of 9th row.
52 [57: 62: 68] sts.
Work 1 row, ending with RS facing for next row.
(Left front should now match back to beg of
armhole shaping.)

Shape armhole
Cast off 3 [4: 5: 6] sts at beg of next row.
49 [53: 57: 62] sts.
Work 1 row.
Dec 1 st at armhole edge of next 1 [3: 3: 5] rows,
then on foll 2 [2: 3: 3] alt rows **and at same
time** dec 1 st at front slope edge of next and
every foll 4th row.
44 [46: 48: 51] sts.
Dec 1 st at front slope edge **only** on 4th [2nd:
4th: 2nd] and every foll 4th row to 32 [35: 37: 41]
sts, then on 0 [1: 1: 2] foll 6th rows.
32 [34: 36: 39] sts.
Cont straight until left front matches back to beg
of shoulder shaping, ending with RS facing for
next row.
Shape shoulder
Cast off 6 [7: 7: 8] sts at beg of next and foll alt
row, 6 [6: 8: 9] sts at beg of foll alt row, then 5 sts
at beg of foll 2 alt rows.
Work 1 row.
Cast off rem 4 sts.

RIGHT FRONT
Using 5mm (US 8) needles cast on 72 [77: 82: 88] sts.
Row 1 (RS): Purl.
Row 2: Knit.
Beg with a K row, cont in st st, dec 1 st at end of
19th [21st: 25th: 27th] row.
71 [76: 81: 87] sts.
Work 1 row, ending with RS facing for next row.
★★Next row (RS): K62 [66: 70: 75], wrap next st
(by slipping st from left needle onto right needle,
taking yarn to opposite side of work between
needles and then slipping same st back onto left
needle – when working back across wrapped st
work the st and the wrapped loop tog as one st)
and turn.
Next row: Purl.
Next row: K52 [55: 58: 62], wrap next st and turn.
Next row: Purl.
Next row: K42 [44: 46: 49], wrap next st and turn.
Next row: Purl.
Next row: K32 [33: 34: 36], wrap next st and turn.
Next row: Purl.
Next row: K22 [22: 22: 23], wrap next st and turn.
Next row: Purl.★★
Cont in st st across all sts, dec 1 st at end of
19th row.
70 [75: 80: 86] sts.
Work 5 rows, ending with RS facing for next row.
Rep from ★★ to ★★ once more.

Work 2 rows, ending with RS facing for next row.
Shape front slope
Dec 1 st at beg of next and foll 13 alt rows **and at
same time** inc 1 st at end of 9th row.
57 [62: 67: 73] sts.
Work 1 row, ending with RS facing for next row.
Next row (RS): K13 and slip these sts onto a
holder, K to last st, inc in last st.
45 [50: 55: 61] sts.
Dec 1 st at front slope edge of 2nd and foll 5 [4:
4: 3] alt rows, then on 1 [2: 2: 2] foll 4th rows.
38 [43: 48: 55] sts.
Work 2 [0: 0: 2] rows, ending with **WS** facing for
next row.
Shape armhole
Cast off 3 [4: 5: 6] sts at beg of next row.
35 [39: 43: 49] sts.
Dec 1 st at armhole edge of next 1 [3: 3: 5] rows,
then on foll 2 [2: 3: 3] alt rows **and at same
time** dec 1 st at front slope edge of next [3rd: 3rd:
next] and 1 [1: 1: 2] foll 4th rows.
30 [32: 35: 38] sts.
Dec 1 st at front slope edge **only** on 4th [4th:
2nd: 2nd] and every foll 4th row until 18 [20: 22:
25] sts rem.
Cont straight until right front matches back to beg
of shoulder shaping, ending with **WS** facing for
next row.
Shape shoulder
Cast off 6 [7: 7: 8] sts at beg of next and foll alt row.
Work 1 row.
Cast off rem 6 [6: 8: 9] sts.

SLEEVES
Using 5mm (US 8) needles cast on 60 [62: 64: 64] sts.
Row 1 (RS): Purl.
Row 2: Knit.
Beg with a K row, cont in st st, shaping sides by
inc 1 st at each end of 11th [11th: 9th: 7th] and
every foll 14th [12th: 10th: 8th] row to 76 [74: 68:
68] sts, then on every foll - [14th: 12th: 10th] row
until there are - [80: 84: 88] sts.
Cont straight until sleeve meas 46 [47: 48: 48] cm,
ending with RS facing for next row.
Shape top
Cast off 3 [4: 5: 6] sts at beg of next 2 rows.
70 [72: 74: 76] sts.
Keeping patt correct, dec 1 st at each end of next
13 rows, then on every foll alt row to 38 sts, then
on foll 5 rows, ending with RS facing for next
row. 28 sts.
Cast off 9 sts at beg of next 2 rows.

Cast off rem 10 sts.

MAKING UP
Press as described on the information page.
Join both shoulder seams using back stitch, or
mattress stitch if preferred and leaving front
opening edge 14 sts free at neck edge of left front.
Left front edging
With RS facing and using 5mm (US 8) needles,
beg at neck cast-off edge of left front, pick up and
knit 69 [71: 73: 75] sts down left front slope to beg
of front slope shaping, then 46 [48: 49: 51] sts
down left front opening edge to cast-on edge.
115 [119: 122: 126] sts.
Cast off knitwise (on **WS**).
Right front band
Slip 13 sts from right front holder onto 5mm
(US 8) needles and rejoin yarn with **WS** facing.

58 [60: 62: 64] cm
(23 [23½: 24½: 25] in)

47 [52: 57.5: 63.5] cm
(18½ [20½: 22½: 25] in)

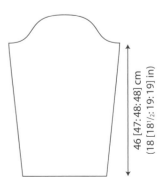

46 [47: 48: 48] cm
(18 [18½: 19: 19] in)

Row 1 (WS): Inc in first st, (K2, inc in next st) 4 times.
18 sts.
Row 2: K2, (P2, K2) 4 times.
Row 3: (P2, K2) 4 times, P1, K1.
Rep rows 2 and 3 until band, when slightly stretched, fits up right front slope and across back neck, ending with RS facing for next row.
Cast off.
Join cast-off end of this band to cast-off sts left free at top of left front, then slip stitch band in place.

Right front edging
With RS facing and using 5mm (US 8) needles, beg at cast-on edge of right front, pick up and knit 48 [49: 52: 53] sts up right front opening edge to beg of front slope shaping, then 23 sts up right front slope to beg of ribbed section.
71 [72: 75: 76] sts.
Cast off knitwise (on **WS**).
See information page for finishing instructions, setting in sleeves using the set-in method.

Ties (both alike)
Using 5.00mm (US H8) crochet hook, make a ch approx 30 cm long.
Row 1: 1 dc into 2nd ch from hook, 1 dc into each ch to end.
Fasten off.
Attach end of one tie to right front opening edge and end of other tie to left side seam, attaching both ties level with beg of front slope shaping.

SAKURA
BY MARIE WALLIN
MAIN IMAGE PAGE 16 & 26

SIZE

	S	M	L	XL	
To fit bust					
	82-87	92-97	102-107	112-117	cm
	32-34	36-38	40-42	44-46	in

YARN
Rowan Bamboo

10	12	13	15	x 50gm

(photographed in Rope 706)

NEEDLES
1 pair 5mm (no 6) (US 8) needles
5.00mm (no 6) (US H8) crochet hook

TENSION
19 sts and 27 rows to 10 cm measured over stocking stitch using 5mm (US 8) needles.

CROCHET ABBREVIATIONS
ch = chain; **dc** = double crochet.

BACK and FRONT (both alike)
Using 5mm (US 8) needles cast on 86 [96: 106: 118] sts.
Row 1 (RS): Purl.
Beg with a P row, cont in st st, dec 1 st at each end of 14th and every foll 6th row until 78 [88:

98: 110] sts rem.
Work 15 rows, ending with RS facing for next row.
Inc 1 st at each end of next and every foll 8th row until there are 86 [96: 106: 118] sts.
Cont straight until work meas 34 [35: 36: 37] cm, ending with RS facing for next row.

Shape for armholes
Inc 1 st at each end of next 4 rows, ending with RS facing for next row.
94 [104: 114: 126] sts.
Place markers at both ends of last row to denote base of armhole openings.
Inc 1 st at each end of 11th and 2 foll 10th rows.
100 [110: 120: 132] sts.
Cont straight until armhole meas 16 [17: 18: 19] cm **from markers**, ending with RS facing for next row.

Shape shoulders
Dec 1 st at each end of next and foll alt row, then on foll 7 rows, ending with RS facing for next row. 82 [92: 102: 114] sts.
Cast off 9 [12: 14: 17] sts at beg of next 2 rows, then 11 [13: 15: 18] sts at beg of foll 2 rows.
42 [42: 44: 44] sts.

Shape funnel neck
Work 1 row, ending with **WS** facing for next row.
Dec 1 st at each end of next and foll 3rd row.
38 [38: 40: 40] sts.

Work 1 row, ending with RS facing for next row.
Cast off.

MAKING UP
Press as described on the information page.
Join both shoulder and funnel neck seams using back stitch, or mattress stitch if preferred.

Armhole borders (both alike)
With RS facing and using 5mm (US 8) needles, pick up and knit 71 [75: 79: 83] sts evenly along armhole edge between markers.
Row 1 (WS): Purl.
Cast off knitwise.

Front panel
Using 5.00mm (US H8) hook make 22 ch.
Foundation row (RS): 1 dc into 2nd ch from hook, 1 dc into each ch to end, turn. 21 sts.
Next row: 1 ch (does NOT count as st), 1 dc into each dc to end, turn.
Rep last row until panel meas 36 [41: 47: 53] cm.
Fasten off.
Lay front panel onto RS of Front, matching row-end edge of panel to cast-on edge of front, and foundation ch edge to right side seam row-end edge of front. Join side seams, enclosing front panel in right side seam.
Ties (make 6)
Using 5.00mm (US H8) crochet hook, make a ch approx 40 cm long.

Row 1: 1 dc into 2nd ch from hook, 1 dc into each ch to end.
Fasten off.
Attach ends of 3 ties to free end of front panel as in photograph. Attach ends of rem 3 ties to left side seam to correspond.

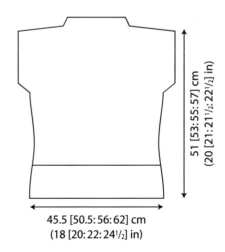

51 [53: 55: 57] cm
(20 [21: 21½: 22½] in)

45.5 [50.5: 56: 62] cm
(18 [20: 22: 24½] in)

TORI

BY MARIE WALLIN

MAIN IMAGE PAGE 8

●

SIZE

8	10	12	14	16	18	

To fit bust

82	87	92	97	102	107	cm
32	34	36	38	40	42	in

YARN

Rowan Bamboo

9	9	9	10	11	12	x 50gm

(photographed in Sweet 701)

NEEDLES

1 pair 5mm (no 6) (US 8) needles

RIBBON – 1 m of narrow satin ribbon

TENSION

19 sts and 27 rows to 10 cm measured over stocking stitch using 5mm (US 8) needles.

BACK

Using 5mm (US 8) needles cast on 82 [86: 90: 96: 102: 106] sts.

Row 1 (RS): Purl.

Row 2: Knit.

Beg with a K row, work in st st, dec 1 st at each end of 9th and every foll 10th row until 74 [78: 82: 88: 94: 98] sts rem.

Work 13 rows, ending with RS facing for next row.

Inc 1 st at each end of next and every foll 8th row until there are 82 [86: 90: 96: 102: 106] sts.

Cont straight until back meas 33 [33: 32: 35: 34: 36] cm, ending with RS facing for next row.

Shape armholes

Cast off 3 [4: 4: 5: 5: 6] sts at beg of next 2 rows.

76 [78: 82: 86: 92: 94] sts.

Dec 1 st at each end of next 1 [1: 3: 3: 5: 5] rows, then on foll 5 [5: 4: 5: 4: 4] alt rows.

64 [66: 68: 70: 74: 76] sts.★★

Cont straight until armhole meas 20 [20: 21: 21: 22: 22] cm, ending with RS facing for next row.

Shape shoulders and back neck

Cast off 5 [6: 6: 6: 7: 7] sts at beg of next 4 rows, then 6 [5: 6: 7: 6: 7] sts at beg of foll 2 rows.

32 [32: 32: 32: 34: 34] sts.

Dec 1 st at each end of next 2 rows, ending with RS facing for next row.

Cast off rem 28 [28: 28: 28: 30: 30] sts.

FRONT

Work as given for back to ★★.

Cont straight until 31 [31: 33: 33: 37: 37] rows less have been worked than on back to beg of shoulder shaping, ending with **WS** facing for next row.

Shape front slope

Cast off 4 sts at beg of next row, 3 [4: 3: 4: 3: 4] sts at beg of foll alt row, then 3 sts at beg of foll alt row, ending with RS facing for next row.

54 [55: 58: 59: 64: 65] sts.

Dec 1 st at front slope edge of next 26 [26: 28: 28: 32: 32] rows, ending with RS facing for next row.

28 [29: 30: 31: 32: 33] sts.

Shape shoulder

Cast off 5 [6: 6: 6: 7: 7] sts at beg of next and foll alt row, then 6 [5: 6: 7: 6: 7] sts at beg of foll alt row **and at same time** dec 1 st at front slope edge on every row.

7 sts.

Dec 1 st at front slope edge of next row.

6 sts.

Dec 1 st at each end of next 2 rows, ending with RS facing for next row.

Next row (RS): K2tog and fasten off.

RIGHT FRONT SHOULDER PANEL

Using 5mm (US 8) needles cast on 4 sts.
Beg with a K row, work in st st as folls:
Work 2 rows, ending with RS facing for next row.
Cast on 3 [4: 3: 4: 3: 4] sts at beg of next row, then 3 sts at beg of foll alt row.
10 [11: 10: 11: 10: 11] sts.
Work 1 row, ending with RS facing for next row.
Inc 1 st at beg of next row and at same edge on foll 21 [21: 23: 23: 26: 26] rows.
32 [33: 34: 35: 37: 38] sts.

Shape front slope
Dec 1 st at shaped edge of next 5 [5: 5: 5: 6: 6] rows, ending with **WS** facing for next row.
27 [28: 29: 30: 31: 32] sts.

Shape shoulder
Cast off 5 [6: 6: 6: 7: 7] sts at beg of next and foll alt row, then 6 [5: 6: 7: 6: 7] sts at beg of foll alt row **and at same time** dec 1 st at front slope edge on every row.
6 sts.
Dec 1 st at each end of next 2 rows, ending with RS facing for next row.
Next row (RS): K2tog and fasten off.

SLEEVES

Using 5mm (US 8) needles cast on 51 [53: 55: 57: 59: 61] sts.
Row 1 (RS): Purl.
Row 2: Knit.
Beg with a K row, work in st st for 8 rows, ending

with RS facing for next row.

Shape top
Cast off 3 [4: 4: 5: 5: 6] sts at beg of next 2 rows.
45 [45: 47: 47: 49: 49] sts.
Dec 1 st at each end of next and foll 4 alt rows, then on 3 foll 4th rows, then on every foll alt row until 15 sts rem.
Work 1 row, ending with RS facing for next row.
Cast off 5 sts at beg of next 2 rows.
Cast off rem 5 sts.

MAKING UP

Press as described on the information page.
Join both shoulder seams using back stitch, or mattress stitch if preferred.

Neck edging
With RS facing and using 5mm (US 8) needles, pick up and knit 11 [11: 11: 11: 12: 12] sts up front slope of right front shoulder panel, 28 [28: 28: 28: 30: 30] sts from back, then 44 [45: 46: 47: 50: 51] sts down left front slope, ending at armhole edge. 83 [84: 85: 86: 92: 93] sts.
Cast off knitwise (on **WS**).
Lay front over right front shoulder panel so that pick-up row of front neck edging matches shaped row-end edge of right front shoulder panel and sew together for 7 cm from armhole edge.
See information page for finishing instructions, setting in sleeves using the set-in method. Cut ribbon into 3 equal lengths. Using photograph as a guide, thread each length of ribbon through neck

opening edge, positioning one piece at end of seam, another piece at base of neck and third piece halfway between. Tie ribbons in bows to fasten neck.

43 [45.5: 47.5: 50.5: 53.5: 56] cm
(17 [18: 18½: 20: 21: 22] in)

53 [53: 53: 56: 56: 58] cm
(21 [21: 21: 22: 22: 23] in)

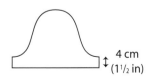

4 cm
(1½ in)

CROCHET STITCHES

Although the crochet effects used within these designs may seem daunting to the beginner, they are actually very simple and use the very basic crochet stitches.

We hope this article will explain the basic stitches needed to complete the designs within Bamboo Tape Collection, and encourage everyone to pick up a crochet hook and 'have a go'. You will be surprised how easy it is and once you have mastered the basics, you can then go onto create some beautiful effects.

MAKING A CHAIN STITCH (CH) AND FOUNDATION CHAIN.

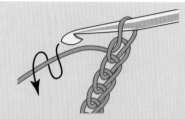

1. All crochet is started by making a slip knot in exactly the same way as you would begin knitting. Slip this knot onto the crochet hook and you're ready to make your first foundation chain. As when knitting, this slip knot is your first stitch.

2. Hold the crochet hook in your right hand and grip the base of the slip knot between the thumb and first finger of the left hand. Wind the ball end of the yarn (working) around the fingers of your left hand to control the tension – exactly as you would when knitting but on the other hand. To make the first **chain**, twist the hook back and under the working strand of yarn so that it loops around the hook. Pull this new loop of yarn through the loop already on the hook and you have made another chain.

3. Continue in this way, drawing new loops of yarn through the loop on the hook, until you have made the required number of chains.

MAKING A SLIP STITCH (SS).

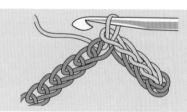

1. A **slip stitch** is the very shortest and easiest of the basic stitches. To work a slip stitch, insert the hook into the work and take the yarn over the hook in the same way as if you were going to make a chain stitch. Pull this new loop of yarn through both the work and the loop on the hook – this completes the slip stitch.

MAKING A DOUBLE CROCHET (DC) AMERICAN SINGLE CROCHET (SC)

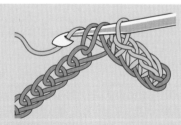
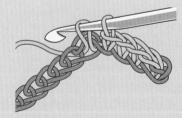
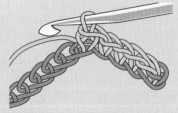

1. The next tallest stitch, the **double crochet** is one of the two most commonly used crochet stitches. This is worked in a similar way to a slip stitch. Start by inserting the hook into the work, and taking the yarn over the hook.

2. Draw this new loop through just the work, leaving two loops on the hook.

3. Take the yarn over the hook again. Draw this new loop through both the loops on the hook thereby completing the double crochet stitch.

MAKING A TREBLE (TR) AMERICAN DOUBLE CROCHET (DC)

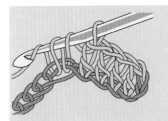 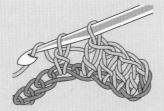  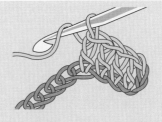

1. The other most commonly used crochet stitch is the **treble**. To make a treble start by taking the yarn over the hook BEFORE inserting into the work.

2. Then insert the hook into the work, take

the yarn over the hook again and draw this new loop through. There are now three loops on the hook.

3. Take the yarn over the hook and draw this new loop through the first two loops only

on the hook. There are now two loops on the hook.

4. Take the yarn over the hook, and draw this through the remaining two loops on the hook to complete the treble stitch.

MAKING A DOUBLE TREBLE (DTR) AMERICAN TREBLE (TR)

1. The taller **double treble** is worked as for the treble, except that the yarn is wrapped around the hook twice before it is inserted into the work. To begin take the yarn twice round the hook. Insert the hook into the work, take the yarn over the hook and draw through the work. There are now four loops on the hook. Take the yarn over the

hook and draw through the first two loops only on the hook. There are now three loops on the hook. Continue taking the yarn over the hook and drawing through two loops at a time until just one loop remains. The double treble is now complete.

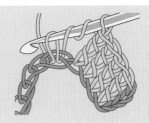

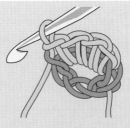

WORKING IN ROUNDS.

  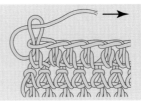

1. To start a piece of circular crochet, begin by making the foundation chain. Now secure the ends of this chain to each other by working a slip stitch into the first chain to form a loop.

2. Make sure you don't twist the chain before you join the ends as this could make the work

twisted or the stitches uneven. The first 'round' of crochet is worked into the ring. The instructions in the pattern will tell you which stitches and how many need to be worked.

3. At the end of each round you will need to secure the last stitch to the first stitch to close

the round. Do this by working a slip stitch into the top of the first stitch. Also in following rounds the stitches need to be raised, this is done by working twice into the same stitch were instructed. The work is not turned at the end of a round, so the right side is always facing you.

FASTENING OFF.

To fasten off your crochet work, cut the yarn about 8cm from the work. Pass this loose end through the one remaining loop

on the hook and pull tight. Darn the loose ends into the back of the work, using a blunt ended needle.

INFORMATION

TENSION

Obtaining the correct tension is perhaps the single factor which can make the difference between a successful garment and a disastrous one. It controls both the shape and size of an article, so any variation, however slight, can distort the finished garment. Different designers feature in our books and it is **their** tension, given at the **start** of each pattern, which you must match. We recommend that you knit a square in pattern and/or stocking stitch (depending on the pattern instructions) of perhaps 5 - 10 more stitches and 5 - 10 more rows than those given in the tension note. Mark out the central 10cm square with pins. If you have too many stitches to 10cm try again using thicker needles, if you have too few stitches to 10cm try again using finer needles. Once you have achieved the correct tension your garment will be knitted to the measurements indicated in the size diagram shown at the end of the pattern.

SIZING & SIZE DIAGRAM NOTE

The instructions are given for the smallest size. Where they vary, work the figures in brackets for the larger sizes. **One set of figures refers to all sizes.** Included with most patterns in this brochure is a 'size diagram', or sketch of the finished garment and its dimensions. The size diagram shows the finished width of the garment at the under-arm point, and it is this measurement that the knitter should choose first; a useful tip is to measure one of your own garments which is a comfortable fit. Having chosen a size based on width, look at the corresponding length for that size; if you are not happy with the total length which we recommend, adjust your own garment before beginning your armhole shaping -

any adjustment after this point will mean that your sleeve will not fit into your garment easily - don't forget to take your adjustment into account if there is any side seam shaping. Finally, look at the sleeve length; the size diagram shows the finished sleeve measurement, taking into account any top-arm insertion length. Measure your body between the centre of your neck and your wrist, this measurement should correspond to half the garment width plus the sleeve length. Again, your sleeve length may be adjusted, but remember to take into consideration your sleeve increases if you do adjust the length - you must increase more frequently than the pattern states to shorten your sleeve, less frequently to lengthen it.

FINISHING INSTRUCTIONS

After working for hours knitting a garment, it seems a great pity that many garments are spoiled because such little care is taken in the pressing and finishing process. Follow the following tips for a truly professional-looking garment.

PRESSING

Block out each piece of knitting and following the instructions on the ball band press the garment pieces, omitting the ribs. Tip: Take special care to press the edges, as this will make sewing up both easier and neater. If the ball band indicates that the fabric is not to be pressed, then covering the blocked out fabric with a damp white cotton cloth and leaving it to stand will have the desired effect. Darn in all ends neatly along the selvage edge or a colour join, as appropriate.

STITCHING

When stitching the pieces together,

remember to match areas of colour and texture very carefully where they meet. Use a seam stitch such as back stitch or mattress stitch for all main knitting seams and join all ribs and neckband with mattress stitch, unless otherwise stated.

CONSTRUCTION

Having completed the pattern instructions, join left shoulder and neckband seams as detailed above. Sew the top of the sleeve to the body of the garment using the method detailed in the pattern, referring to the appropriate guide:
Shallow set-in sleeves: Match decreases at beg of armhole shaping to decreases at top of sleeve. Sew sleeve head into armhole, easing in shapings.
Set- in sleeves: Place centre of cast-off edge of sleeve to shoulder seam. Set in sleeve, easing sleeve head into armhole.

Join side and sleeve seams.
Slip stitch pocket edgings and linings into place.
Sew on buttons to correspond with buttonholes.
Ribbed welts and neckbands and any areas of garter stitch should not be pressed.

Running stitch

ABBREVIATIONS

K	knit	**alt**	alternate	**yfwd**	yarn forward
P	purl	**cont**	continue	**meas**	measures
st(s)	stitch(es)	**patt**	pattern	**0**	no stitches, times or rows
inc	increas(e)(ing)	**tog**	together	**-**	no stitches, times or rows for that size
dec	decreas(e)(ing)	**mm**	millimetres		
st st	stocking stitch (1 row K, 1 row P)	**cm**	centimetres	**approx**	approximately
g st	garter stitch (K every row)	**in(s)**	inch(es)	**m1**	make one stitch by picking up horizontal loop before next stitch and knitting into back of it
beg	begin(ning)	**RS**	right side		
foll	following	**WS**	wrong side		
rem	remain(ing)	**sl 1**	slip one stitch		
rev st st	reverse stocking stitch (1 row P, 1 row K)	**psso**	pass slipped stitch over	**yfrn**	yarn forward round needle
		tbl	through back of loop	**yon**	yarn over needle
rep	repeat	**yrn**	yarn round needle		

EXPERIENCE RATINGS

● Easy, straight forward knitting / crocheting

●● Suitable for the average knitter / crocheter

●●● For the more experienced knitter

Photographer Gisella Torres • Stylists Marie Wallin & Sarah Hatton • Hair & Make-up Jeni Dodson • Models Martha at M & P Models • Design Layout Simon Wagstaff

With special thanks to the following handknitters:
Jenni Shore, Kath Gill, Margaret Gaoddard, Ann Holdsworth, Marie Donachy, Jenny Cooper, Mrs Pickering, Yvonne Rawlinson, Ella Taylor, Andrea McHugh, Audrey Kidd, Fiona McCabe, Anne Banks.

With Special thanks to Diwan Production company

First published in Great Britain in 2006 by Rowan Yarns Ltd, Green Lane Mill, Holmfirth, West Yorkshire, England, HD9 2DX
Internet: www.knitrowan.com
© Copyright Rowan 2007
British Library Cataloguing in Publication Data Rowan Yarns - The Bamboo Tape Collection
ISBN 1-904485-93-6

STOCKISTS

AUSTRALIA: Australian Country Spinners, 314 Albert Street, Brunswick, Victoria 3056
Tel: (61) 3 9380 3888 Fax: (61) 3 9387 2674
E-mail: sales@auspinners.com.au

AUSTRIA: Coats Harlander GmbH, Autokaderstrasse 31, A -1210 Wien.
Tel: (01) 27716 – 0   Fax : (01) 27716 - 228

BELGIUM: Pavan, Meerlaanstraat 73, B9860 Balegem (Oosterzele).
Tel: (32) 9 221 8594   Fax: (32) 9 221 8594
E-mail: pavan@pandora.be

CANADA: Diamond Yarn, 9697 St Laurent, Montreal, Quebec, H3L 2N1
Tel: (514) 388 6188

Diamond Yarn (Toronto), 155 Martin Ross, Unit 3, Toronto, Ontario, M3J 2L9
Tel: (416) 736 6111   Fax: (416) 736 6112
E-mail: diamond@diamondyarn.com
Internet: www.diamondyarn.com

DENMARK: Coats Danmark A/S, Marienlunds Allé 4, 7430 Ikast
Tel: (45) 96 60 34 00
Fax: (45) 96 60 34 08
Email: coats@coats.dk

FINLAND: Coats Opti Oy, Ketjutie 3, 04220 Kerava
Tel: (358) 9 274 871 Fax: (358) 9 2748 7330
E-mail: coatsopti.sales@coats.com

FRANCE: Coats France / Steiner Frères, 100, avenue du Général de Gaulle, 18 500 Mehun-Sur-Yèvre
Tel: (33) 02 48 23 12 30   Fax: (33) 02 48 23 12 40

GERMANY: Coats GMbH, Kaiserstrasse 1, D-79341 Kenzingen
Tel: (49) 7644 8020   Fax: (49) 7644 802399
Internet: www.coatsgmbh.de

HOLLAND: de Afstap, Oude Leliestraat 12, 1015 AW Amsterdam
Tel: (31) 20 6231445 Fax: (31) 20 427 8522

HONG KONG: East Unity Co Ltd, Unit B2, 7/F Block B, Kailey Industrial Centre, 12 Fung Yip Street, Chai Wan
Tel: (852) 2869 7110 Fax: (852) 2537 6952
E-mail: eastuni@netvigator.com

ICELAND: Storkurinn, Laugavegi 59, 101 Reykjavik Tel: (354) 551 8258
E-mail: malin@mmedia.is

ITALY: D.L. srl, Via Piave, 24 – 26, 20016 Pero, Milan
Tel: (39) 02 339 10 180   Fax: (39) 02 33914661

JAPAN: Puppy-Jardin Co Ltd, 3-8-11 Kudanminami Chiyodaku, Hiei Kudan Bldg. 5F, Tokyo. Tel: (81) 3 3222-7076 Fax: (81) 3 3222- 7066
E-mail: info@rowan-jaeger.com

KOREA: Coats Korea Co Ltd, 5F Kuckdong B/D, 935-40 Bangbae- Dong, Seocho-Gu, Seoul
Tel: (82) 2 521 6262. Fax: (82) 2 521 5181

LEBANON: y.knot, Saifi Village, Mkhalissiya Street 162, Beirut,
Tel: (961) 1 992211. Fax: (961) 1 315553.
E-mail: y.knot@cyberia.net.lb

NEW ZEALAND: Please contact Rowan for details of stockists

NORWAY: Coats Knappehuset AS, Pb 100 Ulste, 5873 Bergen
Tel: (47) 55 53 93 00   Fax: (47) 55 53 93 93

SINGAPORE: Golden Dragon Store, 101 Upper Cross Street #02-51, People's Park Centre, Singapore 058357   Tel: (65) 6 5358454 Fax : (65) 6 2216278
E-mail: gdscraft@hotmail.com

SOUTH AFRICA: Arthur Bales PTY, PO Box 44644, Linden 2104
Tel: (27) 11 888 2401 Fax: (27) 11 782 6137

SPAIN: Oyambre, Pau Claris 145, 80009 Barcelona.
Tel: (34) 670 011957 Fax: (34) 93 4872672
E-mail: oyambre@oyambreonline.com

SWEDEN: Coats Expotex AB, Division Craft, Box 297, 401 24 Goteborg
Tel: (46) 33 720 79 00 Fax: 46 31 47 16 50

SWITZERLAND: Coats Stroppel AG, CH -5300 Turgi (AG) .
Tel: (41) 562981220 Fax: (41) 56 298 12 50

TAIWAN:
Laiter Wool Knitting Co Ltd, 10-1 313 Lane, Sec 3, Chung Ching North Road, Taipei
Tel: (886) 2 2596 0269 Fax : (886) 2 2598 0619

U.S.A.: Westminster Fibers Inc, 4 Townsend West, Suite 8, Nashua, New Hampshire 03063
Tel: (1 603) 886 5041 / 5043 Fax (1 603) 886 1056
E-mail: rowan@westminsterfibers.com

U.K: Rowan, Green Lane Mill, Holmfirth, West Yorkshire, England HD9 2DX
Tel: +44 (0) 1484 681881 Fax: +44 (0) 1484 687920
E-mail: mail@knitrowan.com
Inernet: www.knitrowan.com

For stockists in all other countries please contact Rowan for details.